This journal belongs to

_____

Journal Beyond
& Journey Home

Welcome to the realm of Lemuria, a magical place infused with an abundance of life-force energy, fertile lands, lush rainforests, crystalline waterfalls and beings who so gracefully dance with the tides of nature and the ebb and flow of life. There is no scarcity, as all that is required can be created at will. In essence, Lemuria is an elevated state of being... a dreaming that sees beyond the dream.

Lemuria is the knowing of the Universe and all her stars, the all that came before and ever will be, the iridescent shimmer of remembering what we came here to do, the awakening beyond the veil of the mundane, the journey back to wholeness in honour of every part of who we are. This is the unfurling, back to our hearts, the sovereign incarnation, the interconnectedness of existence. This is home.

WHAT IS LEMURIA?

Many of us are familiar with Atlantis, a lost civilisation that disappeared into the Atlantic Ocean many thousands of years ago. Atlantis was home to a highly evolved race of beings whose technology was centred around the power of crystals. They harnessed natural energy in a way that is currently unfathomable to us.

Also known as Mu, Lemuria was home to another civilisation that existed at the same time or just before Atlantis. Located in the Pacific Ocean, its residents were of a gentler, more earth-based nature. They also worked with the crystalline forces of minerals and the planets. They sought to be in harmony with life rather than the hierarchical power that would push evolution to the threshold and eventually bring extinction across the planet.

Lemuria and Atlantis may have resided in physical reality. There are also accounts that imply these civilisations exist or existed in a multidimensional overlay to the reality with which we are more familiar. Whatever you believe, their lessons, stories and understanding of the universe and the future of humanity is accessible to us.

When we work with the energies of their blueprints, as mythical stories, archetypes or as a reality that is even more true than the physical (and that our indigenous kin may inspire us to see), we can find our way to their wisdom.

There seems to be an influx of Lemurian incarnates on Earth right now. Another view is that the archetypal message these beings carry is showing up in increasing prevalence. There is a remembering and a realisation that the keys for a sustainable future are in the ancient roots of our ancestors and the lost civilisations that came before. You may also be familiar with Lemurian quartz crystals, known as seed crystals. They are found buried in the ground and indented with lines — ridges and furrows. It is said they hold Lemurian wisdom that will one day be significant to a future civilisation.

Right now, we are facing a parallel story of Lemuria and Atlantis. By working against the laws of nature rather than with them, humanity heads toward the possibility of erasing life on Earth. The message of the Lemurians is that we can do it differently this time. The shift starts from within ourselves. As we move through our own trauma, triggers and power struggles, we create space for light and life force. We can build on our true inner-sent power and embrace the possibility of bridging Heaven and Earth.
From this vibration, we have a starting point. By holding the vision, not only can we bring Mama Earth and her civilisations back into balance, but we will create the Eden-like paradise this incredible blue planet can be.

The teachings of the Lemurians are alive in the whisperings of ancient natural places. Use this journal to establish or expand your relationship with them. The artworks contain light codes, imagery and symbolism to attune you to their frequency. Lift your vibration through meditation, dance and whatever brings you into the presence of your heart. Open yourself to the wisdom of Lemuria and further your vibrational journey here within these pages.

- *Izzy Ivy*

You are standing at a gateway into the unknown with trust in your heart,
ancient remembering in your soul, and inner illumination to light the way.

When you take time to do what truly makes you shine each day,
you will light up and bring joy to other people's worlds.

You have access to the seat of creation, the spark of existence,
and the codes that hold the blueprints of who and what we are.

The higher you reach for the Divine and the realms of Spirit,
the more important it is to anchor deeply to the earth.

You are held and have strong foundations for all aspects of life.
With your guard down, you have the tools to ride the waves if you need.
Everything is okay.

All of who you are unites in a point of deep experience.

Let yourself drop into passion, intimacy and loving connection with whatever
you are birthing into the world and with whomever you have chosen
to co-create with.

*The way you live is an art form – a unique expression of yourself. You can
dance through challenge, sing through restriction and paint your reality.*

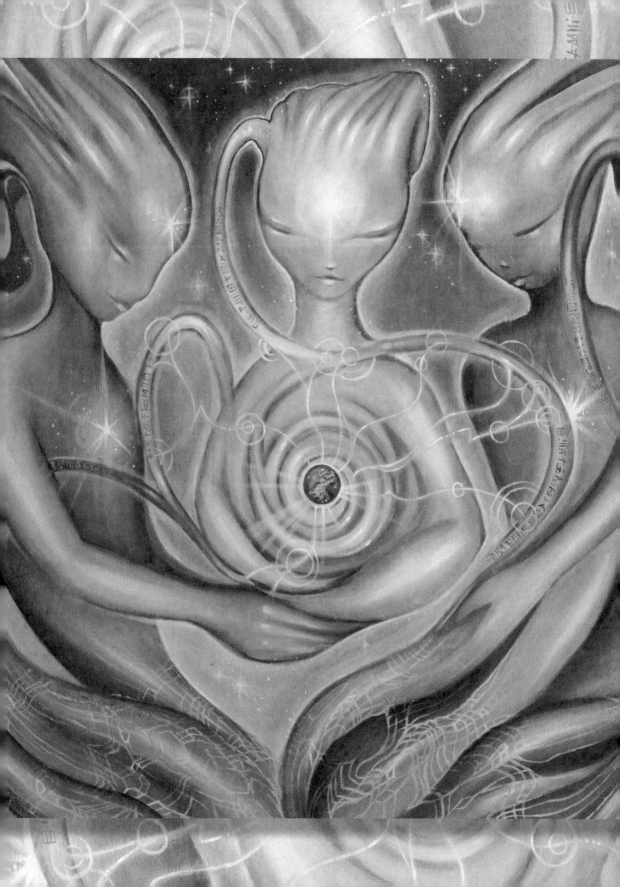

As you discover a deep and real sense of self-empowerment, you can more confidently lift others in celebration, harmonising differences and shifting hierarchical paradigms into collective co-creation.

Remember that you are a powerful being who can connect
with potent life-force energy as and when you need it.

We have lived in many worlds. All interconnected, they uphold the lessons they carry as messages of transformation. Their synergy creates the expansion of the Universe. Gaze into the place where the light between our stardust can become anything, and collective evolution is part of a grander story. When we simply let go, we become all that we have been seeking and glimpse the greater dream.

Everything in life can unfold into love or fear. When unfurled back enough, the foundation of all you seek lies in the universal desire and right to feel love and be loved. Love heals. God is love. This is the force that will change the world.

*When we share our vulnerabilities with others, we allow them to glimpse
a deeper part of ourselves. This is fertile soil for trust. It plants the seeds for
others to share the places that are most raw or tender for them.
Our closest friendships can be formed in this space.*

When we are truly honest with ourselves, in all our facets, we are vulnerable. That honesty is an important step in discovering our shadows and bringing them into the light for healing.

Expand your awareness and heart-centred radiance for all beings on the planet —
encapsulate Earth in loving compassion. Bask in the blissful feeling of the planet,
in all of its perfect balance, loving you back.

Consider your life purpose by exploring what allows you to give in joy.

Humans are evolving, and children can be our wisest teachers.
May we listen to them with our hearts and let their ways
unveil fresh new eyes so we may see a whole new world.

Flow into oneness, where the eternal part of me meets the eternal part of you. This is the selfless state where our higher selves commune for illuminated perspective on how we share, gift and lift others in our joyful overflow.

*This is the outer sharing of our inner being... the glowing song of our soul,
on the winds of our flight to understanding more of who we are.*

This is the place between worlds, the womb before we incarnate, and from here, we can choose where we go. The land has been tilled in readiness for the flowers we wish to seed, outdated doors have been closed, and in the space between the breaths, we open the new ones.

As spirit fuses into the tangible, it actualises as a platform for greater experience and new facets are sculpted, seeded and shared as a fractal of light in the form of our own unique language.

*Be the observant witness, allow the transcendence of duality,
without judgement. Be mindful, listen and allow your unfurling
intuition to unravel the paradoxes of reality.*

*Explore the state of flow and be receptive to the
intuitive messages you may receive.*

In this place of graceful surrender, we may know we are held and allow ourselves the spaciousness to drop deeper into the experience of our existence.

Her heart is also overflowing, with love. Her eyes are filled with tears.
She allows what comes through to move her, without control.
She gracefully allows whatever she is feeling to be expressed
and as she does so, she radiates so much light into the world.

As we wake up, we can't help but awaken those around us.

When the foundations we build on come from a place of love over fear,
we will see huge positive changes in the world.

Just as plastics and oils cannot be broken down in the earth for renewal, when our emotions become hardened and impenetrable, catalysed into something more destructive, they cannot be transformed into the compost that we grow from.

What may be perceived as the endless, black nothingness is actually the illuminated eternal – the core that all our fears may be peeled back to. When we step through the darkness, we realise it is only a short distance away from the white void at the centre of creation and Heaven.

Nature is all around us.
Notice her and know that when you feel like no one else can hold you, she can.

By accepting and loving all of ourselves as we truly are, we can extend more of this love and have deeper compassion with others.

Love is the root of happiness. When we can fluidly give and
receive with the ease of breathing in and out, we can fly freely.

Unconditional love transcends duality. It sees beyond reasoning and situation to allow new stories to be told and for new beginnings to emerge. It transmutes all that is out of balance back to zero point and bridges heaven and earth.

A single glimpse of the limitless eternal and your life will never be the same again. When we directly experience the transient yet profound moment of existence, we can allow the constructs we have spent our lives believing to drop away.

When we walk behind the veil, we discover our true path.

Our affirmations are potent, our prayers are heard and the medicine of life lessons, however strong and uncomfortable, is full of powerful growth.

When we want and strive for something, we create more wanting and striving.
When we immerse ourselves in what it is like to already have something,
we will be in the perfect vibration to receive it.

When our heart motivates our desires, whatever we manifest is aligned with love.

What if everything you wanted was right there in front of you? Make the important decision to let go of outdated limitations. What could be the worst that happens? Reach for what you want and know it is closer than you realise.

When you love what you are doing you keep going,
through the failures and disappointments, until you meet success.

Freedom means living as you choose, with your wings and heart open,
able to direct your reality as you want.

When we honour all that came before, our roots are nourished, and we grow with more vitality, vibrancy and life force. We can anchor more light for the collective, and in turn, seed new growth.

*Be grounded, find your home, as just like a tree, the deeper our roots,
the higher we can reach into the heavens.*

When we stop looking outside ourselves and surrender to a soft inner focus,
we have access to unlimited information and resources. When we stop thinking
with the glass ceiling of our intellect, we have access to multidimensional wisdom
from the collective consciousness.

When we choose to journey through life from our hearts,
it illuminates the darkness, all illusion drops away, and we see what is real.

*What happens when we realise the keys to our future
are in the wisdom of the earth and the dreamings of the indigenous?
That the answers are in the geometry of the macro and microcosm,
the nurturing embrace of oneness, in Mama Nature's arms?
What happens when we find peace within the full spectrum of life?*

When our core foundations are integrity and kindness, our choices are ethical,
and our souls radiate warmth, hold compassionate space for others,
and inspire others to carry it forward.

As we make the journey to wholeness, we see that the parts we have severed from ourselves are counterparts to our greatest strengths.

There is nothing that makes us shine more than a heart that is full of love.
You can shine through the shadows most gracefully when there is no fear within.
Accept your shadows so they can more easily resolve. Allow more light and love,
inside and out of your world.

It is time to dream outside the box. It is time for the inventors, the artists, the poets, and the visionary leaders to step forward and collectively dream in a new future.

Accepting our shadows is the first stage in restoring ourselves to wholeness, in self-love. Peel back the layers where there is shame, guilt or fear and bring them into the daylight. Under a loving and compassionate light, they will resolve and reassimilate so you can re-engage with your superpowers.